21 Ways to Boost Your Business Profits

Using Mobile, Video Marketing & Social Media Tools

http://www.
BoostYourBusinessProfitsUsingMobileVideoMarketingSocialMed
ia.com/

Elaine V. Albright

With

David Albright

About The Authors

Elaine V. Albright Having lived in Silicon Valley, Elaine has loved and been involved in the internet for over 2 decades. She is a Teacher, Speaker and Advisor both domestically and internationally for more than 45 years. She prides in helping businesses small and large to leverage the internet to gain more profits day after day. She does this by showing you how to solve this by broadening your audience through easy to implement tactics both on the internet and offline. She relates this to you by giving the answers to the challenges and opportunities of the new economy. You will learn the powers of these techniques and how the big companies are overcoming this economic struggle. You can too!

David Albright has a record of successfully building and participating in the management of organizations over the last 14 years. His experience of starting, owning and operating small businesses along with extensive advertising both online and offline has generated success. With his extensive background, this gives him the ability to bring a wealth of knowledge to the table with Internet Marketing.

About This Book

Imagine … your advertising being available on every Mobile Phone, IPad, IPhone Blackberry, etc. out there through your Mobile Website. You will have your own Billboard 24/7! Yes, you'll have 24 hour connection to your audience, with no one standing between you and them. With 65% of the searches being done from a Mobile device, if your site is optimized, do you realize what this can do for you and your business' bottom line?

You've actually got a system and it shows up instantly, each time you launch something new on your site. You are "The Billboard", but not one someone zooms by on the freeway. They actually have time to look at it and read what it says!

Your audience now consumes your material whenever and wherever they choose with their Mobile device. They may be at home, on their lunch break, traveling on an airplane, but with their mobile phone or mobile device, they can view it anywhere.

Internet Marketing has made this all feasible -- and think about time savers, your engagement through Social Media can be accessed while you are waiting for an appointment, waiting for your children, waiting at the dentist, etc. That is the wonderful thing about Mobile Devices, their availability which we all need to socially engage in order to generate more Profits for our business.

Do you remember the old Commodore 64 computers that crawled like a snail? We were delighted to have our Commodore 64 to access the internet! Who could have ever imagined what we would have 30 years later? I've never looked back. I have only been grateful for this incredible technology.

Through this book, I want you to be exposed to the 21st Century methodology of Internet Marketing. I want to share with you its fast pace of change. I want you to see, first hand, the extreme benefit for your business to explode your audience and put more money in your pocket during these times of economic struggles.

Once you have finished reading this book and start implementing some of these methods, I don't think you will look back at the old methods of advertising that you previously used.

These Internet Marketing methods utilizing Video (on your site and YouTube Channel), Mobile Marketing and Social Media Marketing Tools will allow you to get your message out to more people than you can ever imagine and through your communication, gain their trust to be a loyal clients. They will come to know you as a real person, not just as the untouchable store owner or business owner, but a real person. It is all about relationships these days. With this comes Trust and builds you as the Authority in your field. The bottom line is … this brings loyalty to you as well as more business and for more profit than anyone would have guessed! Congratulations! When you have implemented these methodologies, You … have … expanded your audience.

It's been a wild and exciting journey!

So, about this book …

I, too, have asked many questions over the past several years. Questions like:

- What is the benefit of FaceBook?
- What has changed?
- I have a website, isn't that enough?
- Why should I have a Video on my website?
- What is the benefit of a Mobile App for my business?
- What is a Strong and Engaging Call to Action?
- And more …

I have created this book as a quick read reference book. You will find the above questions and 15 others addressed so you can take ACTION implementing these techniques.

Start with Way 1 and even if you take action on only 1 per week, that is a step in the right direction. Over achievers may choose to take 2 per week and step up your progress and profits.

When done, you should realize more money in your pocket … yes, you will see Your Business Profits Boosted through taking ACTION on these 21 Ways!

This book is part of a larger project for Marketing Mobile USA. They have a few tools, right now, which can be used for these various marketing techniques, but nothing written in this book requires that. I do recommend them though to make life more automated.

We may have missed a few things, so do us a favor and register this book (directions to register are on another page). We want to keep you up to date when we change things or perhaps our readers may have ideas they want to share that we can share with you. Our community loves sharing ideas. We welcome your ideas.

Elaine Albright

Auburn, California

21 Ways To Boost Your Business Profits Using Mobile, Video Marketing, & Social Media Tools

March 2014

21 WAYS to

BOOST YOUR BUSINESS PROFITS

USING

MOBILE, VIDEO MARKETING AND

SOCIAL MEDIA TOOLS

http://www.
BoostYourBusinessProfitsUsingMobileVideoMarketingSocialMedia.com/

Big Businesses Implement These Techniques

To Maximize Their

Mobile, Video Marketing & Social Media Advantages! So Can You.

Be Engaged, Embrace Social Media, Be Empowered

And

Be Rewarded by Profiting From These Methodologies.

By: Elaine V. Albright

Co-Author: David Albright

Editorial Director: David Albright

Cover Design: Marketing Mobile USA Staff

Production and Composition: Marketing Mobile USA Staff

Author: Elaine V. Albright

With: David Albright

Library of Congress Control Number: 2014902120

ISBN: **978-0-9914705-0-1**

ISBN: **0991470508**

For special discount information on bulk purchases, please contact

Marketing Mobile USA at 1-530 - 823-0888 or

MarketingMobileUSA@Gmail.com

21 Ways to Boost Your Business Profits Using Mobile, Video Marketing & Social Media Tools

Copyright © 2014 Elaine V. Albright

10556 Combie Road

Suite 6429

Auburn, CA 95602

Support@BoostYourBusinessProfitsUsingMobileVideoMarketingSocialMedia.com

Special Offer / Register This Book

The world of Marketing in this 21st Century has statistically proven to be most effective through the Internet. Yet, it is constantly changing, but you must make a necessary endeavor to be exposed and branded. We want to be sure you are kept current on the latest trends.

Register this book so that we can communicate the most up to date and current trends in both Online Internet Marketing and the Offline Marketing arenas.

- Immediate delivery of "21 Ways to Boost Your Business Profits Using Mobile, Video Marketing and Social Media Tools" in Podcasting format - Free! I want you to really put this knowledge to use so you can benefit from your Profits and have more Free time.

- This Podcast will allow you to learn on the run.

- To keep you updated, we will email you once a month some of the most exciting New Trends of Marketing. (Not more than 2 times a month so not to clog your email box).

To get your Bonuses, send a copy of your receipt to:

Bonuses@BoostYourBusinessProfitsUsingMobileVideoMarketingSocialMedia.com

… and we'll do the rest.

Table of Contents

Introduction

In this book, you will find 21 Effective and Dynamic ways that you can implement Mobile Marketing, Video Marketing and Social Media Tools to quickly Boost Your Business to Increase Profits.

You will learn how to get more sales through my Strategic BluePrint Methodology utilizing Mobile, Video and Social Media to Quickly and Easily attract new and loyal clients!

Now, would you find Value in these Strategic Techniques to make your business more Successful?

I understand how you feel. Those newspaper ads and magazine ads just aren't working anymore… You're working harder and longer hours and profiting less!

Frustrating!

Being from Silicon Valley, I have kept up with the latest technology and utilization of the internet to increase business. Well, technology changes rapidly.

I finally figured out the fastest way to get more clients… So can you!

I have studied and tried different combinations and finally came up with the most effective BluePrint Strategy to quickly get more clients which = more profits.

Once I discovered the right path, I started to see results… fast.

Would you say that was great news for both you and me? How would you like to have this Magic Blueprint to make your business grow quickly?

Here's the key. Most businesses haven't figured out the power of this "Magic BluePrint to More Profits". We are on the cutting edge! Time is of the essence. We need to implement these techniques post haste because Big Businesses are starting to aggressively use this technology and the trend is rapidly expanding.

You don't want to get left behind like Kodak did. Kodak waited too long to incorporate digital technology into their market and they now filed bankruptcy! Don't let this be you.

Don't wait!

Let's be a little mouse in the wall and take a look at your relationship when you do business with someone. Now, analyze this. When you do business with someone new or require their services, why did you choose them? Did you get a mailer? Did you look them up in the yellow pages? Did they call you, soliciting you? Were they high pressure sales people?

Probably not!

There are lots of people still doing that, but generally, people have become Numb to those tactics and immediately say "No".

Let me tell you about my "Magic BluePrint To More Profits". Let's talk about this powerful client getting BluePrint that people will welcome your presence.

Social Media

Yes, Social Media is an untapped Gold Mine!

Yes, that's right. **Social Media** is an untapped **Gold Mine!**

Social media is playing a huge role in the lives of modern professionals and small business owners. Today, the world is getting more and more global while at the same time the use of social media seems to have brought this global power to the local market to attract new customers from their own backyard.

Marketing and branding are two of the most important aspects of Your business — small or big — and traditional media seems to run out of steam when it comes to connecting to a large number of customers. This seems apparent when you consider your DVR that allows you to skip right past TV commercials. Or the fast rise of satellite radio where there are no commercials at all, to the fall of so many newspapers because of the drop in advertising revenues, drop in subscribers, and the increase of consumers reading their news online.

Now that Google has changed their Algorithms and purchased YouTube, the Social Media fanatics swear that it is lightning fast and will outgrow any other media in terms of efficiency, but while you cannot guarantee the level of social media success, it is a powerful force that cannot be ignored.

The craze about Social Media is not because it helps you take your message to millions within a second, but it helps business owners to get a better insight into the needs, requirements and mindsets of their customers while deepening a more personal relationship with them. After all, one of the biggest benefits of Social Media is that it is already happening online.

Being able to insert your message into what is already being talked about makes your message well-received because it is not selling. It is participating and educating your target audience. YOU are positioned as the trusted advisor in your type of business.

Let me say this again because this is very critical: because you are educating your target audience. YOU are positioned as the trusted advisor in your type of business.

Marketing is changing radically. These changes will leave many businesses in the dust if they don't quickly take heed and implement this new technology.

You either have to be positioned perfectly to ride their extraordinary wave that's here, or you'll be swept under by it, and your ability to make money will take a serious hit. If not, vanish entirely.

Fortunately, I am going to show you exactly how to put yourself in the driver's seat as this change sweeps the industry.

You're going to know precisely how to cash in on this change that will kill so many other businesses.

Not to worry, if it sounds intimidating, or you don't know where to start. You can watch my **Marketing How To Video** that lays out the whole system for you.

In approximately 19 minutes, you will see exactly how you can build a relationship with your potential customers.

You can access the video here:

http://www.marketingmobileusa.com/video/

In this book, "21 Ways to Boost Your Business Profits Using Mobile, Video Marketing & Social Media Tools", I'll show you how you can Benefit and Boost your Profits from the most active and free Social Media sites online today.

Before Anything Else - Survey

Please Answer the Following Quick 22 Yes or No Survey Questions to see where Your Marketing Strategy fits in today's Revolutionary Transformation.

1) Have you Claimed your Google Places Directory Spot so you Rank in the top 10 when someone searches for you?
2) Have you Claimed your Yahoo Directory Spot so you Rank in the top 10 when someone searches for you?
3) Have you Claimed your Bing Directory Spot so you Rank in the top 10 when someone searches for you?
4) Are you Listed with Angie's List?
5) Do you have Updates and Coupons on each of these Directories?
6) Are you marketing with Videos?
7) Do you have YOUR very own YouTube Channel with your Videos optimized to the maximum to quickly rank you to a higher position?
8) Does Your Video get lost in the millions of YouTube Videos that are randomly uploaded daily to YouTube?
9) Are you marketing with Product Images?
10) Do you have a Mobile Website for the 65% searching on their Mobile Phones to quickly find your easy to read and navigate website?
11) Most importantly… does the viewer see your Mobile site in the correct size so they will continue to view your site and not bounce to someone else's easier to read? …You don't want your Website like those poor sites that are microscopic and crunched up, do you?
12) Viewers want instant gratification. Isn't that what you want when you go to someone else's website from your phone?
13) Do you want the viewer to stay on your Mobile Website after they arrive?
14) Does your Mobile Website invite your customers to give you reviews and take them directly to YOUR review page on the various Citation sites?
15) Do you know the Power in getting reviews?
16) Do you have a very reasonably priced Mobile App that keeps you in front of the Viewer 24/7? It is an Icon on their Mobile Phone.
17) Do you know that, with your own APP, with 1 TAP of the Icon a customer can call you or go to your website or order their dinner or make an appointment?
18) Do you have Your Billboard up? That is, Do you have Your BUSINESS FACEBOOK page to bring LIKES and TRAFFIC to Your business? It is far less expensive than a Highway Billboard, yet, far more valuable. It takes customers to you while they are searching and cruising the web. The costly Highway Billboard ONLY gives them a glance to catch the information before they speed by that Billboard. Our internet highway

allows them to STOP and look at your information. Isn't that an exciting concept?

19) Do you have a TWITTER page to accelerate your TRAFFIC?

20) Do you have a LINKEDIN page to tell the world who you are and what services or products you have to offer? People want to come to KNOW, LIKE and TRUST you. They want to see a picture of you to come to KNOW you. Do you offer that on an optimized LINKEDIN page?

21) Are your Facebook, Twitter and LinkedIn optimized with keywords, phrases and your Customized QR Code for the utmost exposure?

22) Do YOUR Marketing Strategies fit in the Revolutionary 21st Century or do they fit in the Methods of the 1980's that are getting High Bounce Rates and RAPIDLY losing viewership?

Do you Need Help?

Call US Now for your FREE Marketing Blueprint Strategy Consultation. **530-823-0888** or go to the link below and put your contact information in our contact form. We look forward to Helping You Revolutionize Your Marketing Strategies which will Increase Your Exposure and Increase Your Profits.

www.MarketingMobileUSA.com

www.QRCodePowers.com

Scan the QR Code Below

Way 1

Engage with your Client

Your client wants to know that you are a real person. This is why Social Media is so effective. They see your name and your picture and after a few times, it is like you are an old friend. They come to Know, Like and Trust you.

This is the relationship that you want to cultivate. You are a real person. You are not just the person in the store or business office.

Tom Palmer and Louise Palmer petting the Whale

You have real likes, as they do. Maybe you have a love for horses, or maybe you are a Gourmet cook or maybe you love to go to Mexico to pet the Whales, as I do.

These are the things they like to hear about you. They want to Engage with you as a real live person, not just a store or a business owner.

This is what Social Media is all about!

Way 2

Engage in the Conversation

Belonging to the various Social Media sites is like having a virtual coffee break with your friends. You join in the conversation and post your thoughts on the subject. Also, this is your opportunity to make comments if ever there is a negative remark made about your business. You can nip it in the bud and resolve it before it escalates. Great, isn't it?

You can share information and educate your loyal followers on the products or services of which you are the authority. You are not selling them; you are educating them and sharing your knowledge.

source: coachingsymposium.com

People like to buy BUT,

they don't want to be sold to.

Remember, this is a social. 80% of your conversation should be interesting content and 20% business. If you are constantly talking about your business and buying your products, you will find your followers will lose interest and leave. Again, you *must* be a ***Real Person***.

24

Way 3

You Must First Have a Vision

"Those Who Don't Plan,

Plan to Fail."

To Succeed, you must first have a Vision. You then create the BluePrint. You then embellish on that BluePrint to create your Plan. Next, it is time to Execute that Plan. Finally, we Improve on our Plan. Often, after our first experience, we will need to tweak it and adjust it for maximum performance.

We then repeat and expand on this very process.

Now, the most important question is, "What is your Objective?" … Do you want more Exposure, more Money or more Traffic? Yes, you can choose only 1. Difficult, huh?

The answer you give is **most** important. This is the determining factor that we must use to structure your Campaign.

What do you want? More Exposure, More Money, More Traffic?

Way 4

Build on the 8 Step System Step 1

Step 1 of the 8 Step System

"Google +"… formerly Google Places – Exposure through Geo - Targeting

Google is the information center of the Internet where each of us goes to get the information we need. Can you hear your kids or colleagues say to you, "Google It"?

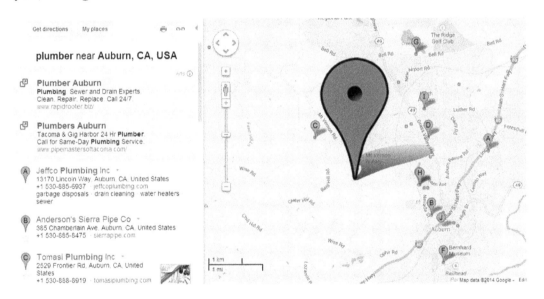

Well, Google Places and now, Google + is where many of the other search engines get their information, such as, Yahoo Places, Bing, and Yelp to mention a few.

When people are out and about, they search from their mobile phone for the particular item that they are considering purchasing.

Are YOU ranked on 1st page of Google Places and Google+ or are you missing out on 65% of the searches done from Mobile Devices? 1st, have you even Claimed your Google Places and Google + pages? Is your Google Places and Google + page fully Optimized to be positioned on the 1st page of Google

Places? 97% of the people searching for a specific item or service that they need do not look further than the 1st page of Google Places.

Is Your business losing Profits because of this?

Do you need to evaluate your

Google Places and Google + Position?

Have YOU Claimed Your pages?

We are Experts in this Arena.

Call for Your Free BluePrint Consultation.

530-823-0888

Way 5

Step 2 of the 8 Step System

Facebook – Extensive Exposure

What is your **Objective?** Do you want **Exposure?** As of August 2012, Facebook has reached 1 BILLION users. How would you like to reach that potential market? With the 2013 population of 316,148,990 people in the United States, Facebook reached about 3 times the size of the United States!

Monthly Active Users (MAUs)

In Millions

- Rest of World
- Asia
- Europe
- US & Canada

	Q2'11	Q3'11	Q4'11	Q1'12	Q2'12	Q3'12	Q4'12	Q1'13	Q2'13
Total	739	800	845	901	955	1,007	1,056	1,110	1,155
Rest of World	183	207	225	245	268	288	304	327	346
Asia	174	196	212	234	255	277	298	319	339
Europe	212	221	229	239	246	253	261	269	272
US & Canada	169	176	179	183	186	189	193	195	198

Source: SocialBakers.com

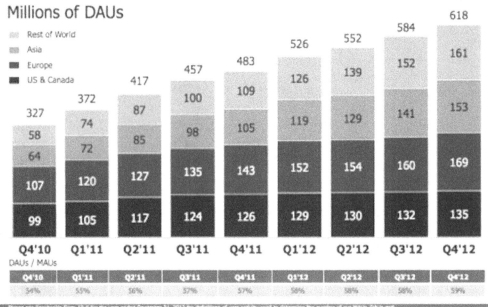

Source: SocialBakers.com

Facebook is a Social Media site you definitely need in your marketing arsenal for more exposure which results in more profits. With Facebook's 1,000,000,000 (1 Billion) users, do you think you just might get Exposure? Yes, that is for sure; if you use it correctly and properly optimize it to its fullest you will increase both Exposure and Profits.

Facebook is a necessary Tool for your business and...it is FREE. It provides a 2 way conversation between customers and your company.

This develops the Know ... Like ... and Trust Factors!

Way 6

Step 3 of the 8 Step System

Twitter – Traffic, Traffic, and more Traffic!

Protecting your Tweets does not allow people to Know … Like and Trust you. Don't check the "Protect my Tweets" box in your Twitter Settings when setting up your Twitter account.

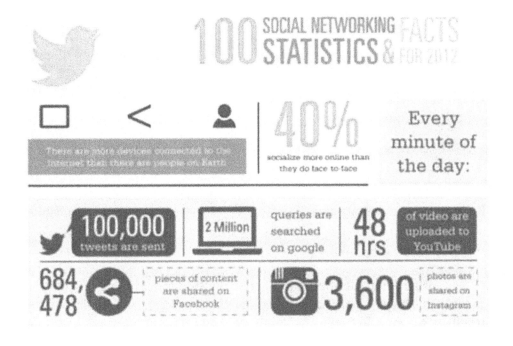

(a)

Source: http://designyoutrust.com/2013/01/100-social-media-statistics-facts-for-2012-infographic/

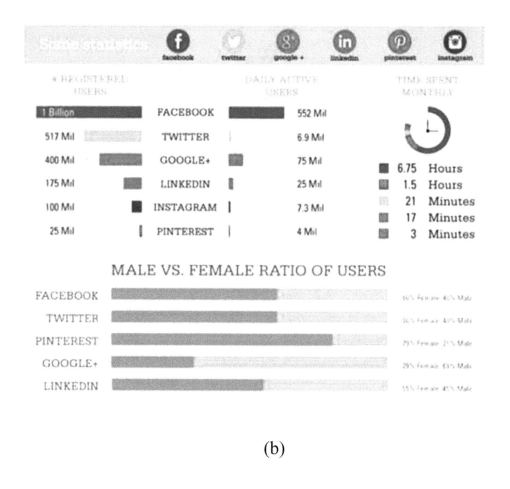

(b)

Using your Mobile with Twitter, Facebook and your Social platforms in general is Huge. You need to build Relationships, and a Community which results in Success.

Create a Custom Branded Background that fits your Marketing Campaign. This establishes effective and efficient branding tools for your Twitter purpose.

Personalize your background to promote your Branding.

Personalize your background to promote your Branding.

As with any marketing campaign, you should monitor your Twitter promotional campaigns by tracking the results. One free way to do this is to use http://search.twitter.com/ to find all instances of people talking about you or your business on Twitter.

Another tool you can use is called Tweet Beep www.TweetBeep.com . This service will automatically email you whenever something is Tweeted about you or your business.

Finally, you can check your website's analytics/traffic statistics program to determine how much traffic you have received from Twitter.

You may want to note that www.Twellow.com is also extremely important to your community. It is basically the Yellow Pages of Twitter. It is One of the **best tools** you have to make Twitter Most effective, efficient and Fun.

Do you want a community that is geographically oriented to deliver your special offers and coupons in order to increase your traffic and profits?

Even Global TV and Global News are using

Facebook and Twitter!

After Building a Twitter account, start immediately using Twitter Search (http://search.twitter.com/) to listen for your name, your competitor's names, words that relate to your space. (Listening always comes first!)

Remember this is a Social time for others to **KNOW – LIKE and TRUST you.**

Ask people about their interests. I know it doesn't sell your products or services but, again, it shows you are human.

Point out interesting things. Contribute content to your followers. If you are boring or always tooting your own horn or pushing your own products, they will drop you. Remember the 80 – 20 Rule. **80% social and 20% business.**

Twitter is a great opinion poll. Ask questions. Twitter is GREAT for getting opinions.

When promoting a blog post, ask a question or explain what's coming next, instead of just dumping a link.

You don't have to read every tweet. You don't have to reply to every @ tweet directed to you (try to reply to some, but don't feel guilty about not replying to all of them). Spend 10-15 minutes a day. Gage your time, but use it wisely.

When you DO talk about your stuff, make it useful. Give content of value to your followers, advice, blog posts, pictures, etc. Remember, a picture is worth a thousand words.

Share the human side of your company. If you're taking time to tweet, it means you believe Social Media has value for human connections. Point us to pictures or videos and other human things.

In the past, it was very hard to observe your customers when they talked casually about your products or about competing products. However, this is exactly what you can accomplish with Twitter by using the Twitter Search Engine properly. You may want to experiment with **Tweetdeck.com** which makes it a lot easier to manage Twitter.

Here's to your success in marketing your business products and services. ☺

Way 7

Step 4 of the 8 Step System

Contests

Contests gain Traffic, Exposure & Brand …

Results = Exploding Your Profits!

Is this something you want for Your business?

We all enjoy winning something. Contests offer an attractive marketing vehicle for small businesses to acquire new clients and create awareness. You don't need to run a billion dollar giveaway like Pepsi, just a valuable prize to your target market.

However, it is important to do Facebook and Twitter Contests the right way. Offer a Prize! Maybe an Ipad or a $500 Gift Certificate or $250 Gift Certificate as a prize, make it valuable. If your business is a car dealership, maybe you choose to give away a Free Car. That will really produce the followers and the potential customers.

The potential customers and the number of followers you get will be very well worth your investment.

What is the 3 letter word for "WORK"? … Right! It is "FUN".

Make it FUN, Build your Relationships, the Know…Like…and Trust Factors.

People LOVE to Win!

This type of campaign creation is good for the down town Ice Cream Store or a Major Corporation. People LOVE to Win whether it is a $100 gift certificate from the Ice Cream Store or a FREE CAR from the Car Dealership or Casino!

One great example is how Universal Studios get massive traffic and leads with 'activity contests' on their Facebook Fanpage, now called TimeLine.

Source: Universal Studios Contest

Great idea to get exposure and to build a huge list of people interested in your particular product. Yes, a list of people that are actually interested in what you have to offer.

With Universal's Contest, Everyone won a Reward! Plus a chance to win $1,000,000 by purchasing a specially marked Universal 100th Aniversary DVD or Blu-ray. Yes, they won 1 of 100's of prizes or a discount and a chance to win the $1,000,000 prize.

How would you like to get in front of 1,000,000,000 (1 Billion) people? Would you like to have that Crowd building traffic and leads for you in a Fun and exciting way? When that crowd engages in your Contest online, it builds your exposure!

Click to click marketing Invigorates and Aplodes the Viral effect when people enter an exciting contest. Their enthusiasm and excitement naturally inspires them to share the contest with family and friends. This creates Community building which is of utmost importance. This spiraling viral effect quickly helps expose Your Brand and Your Business.

So, the Key point to remember and take with you is … Contest gain TRAFFIC, EXPOSURE & BRAND which results in Exploding YOUR Profits!

Way 8

Step 5 of the 8 Step System

Create a Video Tutorial Series

On

YouTube

There are many ways in which you can use YouTube improperly, consequently getting no promotional "juice" resulting from it at all.

In fact, that is the outcome that most businesses experience when they try to make money from YouTube or video content in general.

But here is one way that you can leverage the promotional power of YouTube and the viral nature of video marketing, and experience a traffic surge to your business's website.

Everyone loves to watch Videos! Sharing Content on YouTube is absolutely essential to your Brand. Your viewer has a very short attention span. Keep it short, 1 ½ to 3 minutes.

"Money is plentiful for those who understand the simple laws which govern its acquisition." (George Clason)

Well, here's one of those laws:

Online Video gets MORE Money than ANYTHING. **Yes, more Money than ANYTHING!**

Right now, Online Video Marketing is the easiest, cheapest, and yes - fastest way to attract traffic to your site… AND Video Marketing is an absolute proven KILLER conversion creator and sales getting machine.

What you want to do is to create a tutorial video series. This could be something like a 5- video "How To" series, with each video covering a different topic in an area related to your business. (Secret! You can even do this on GOOGLE HANGOUTS.)

In the very beginning of your video description, be sure to include the full URL to your company's website. This will show up as a "clickable" link once the video is published to YouTube, which will send viewers to your website or lead capture page for more information about how you can help them.

If the videos are well-made and you promote them well, there's a good chance you could see a viral effect. This means that other people will begin referring friends to your videos without any compensation for doing so.

Video is One of the Strategies that Get a High Return on Your Investment

For Both Small and Large Businesses.

The internet's second most popular search engine can be a tough Tube to crack, but not with our advanced team of **Video** SEOs and marketers. We have a specific **Blueprint** for successful Video campaigns.

What is your objective and goal with your **Video**? With that we can then target our specific audience with related keywords. Are we going to direct them to your website to capture their name and email address or are we going to send them to your **FaceBook** Business Page to capture their information and go viral by reaching their friends as well? Again, it is back to focusing on the fundamentals … Your **O**bjective and **G**oal.

Small businesses are beginning to realize the **V**alue of **V**ideo in their websites, exposure on **YouTube**, with their own Video Channel, as well as other **S**ocial **M**edia sites. Over the past year, they have been racing to get their websites **video-capable** by eliminating flash for mobile users. Those same small businesses are also spending more on paid search advertising.

According to a new report, small business advertisers spent more than twice as much on paid search last year. With business owners becoming more savvy about **Internet Marketing,** nearly 4 times as many of them reported, now having video on their website vs. a year ago.

If you don't already have it, Get VIDEO on your website. There's not a single business that can't find a way to use **V**ideo to improve customer relations, branding, and profits. When small businesses are racing to get their **websites video-capable**, you know it has officially moved from gimmicky entertainment to a legitimate business tool.

When you get eyes on your product it produces results. Let's face it, in our Fast Pace world, we would much rather watch a video than read information.

Video Marketing is the bomb when it comes to Google. That's probably why Google bought YouTube. Google just loves video marketing - and detects it to rank your Website, FaceBook Fan Page, now TimeLine, Google Places and Google + higher in the search engines. Google has created Google HANGOUTS to make it easy to produce video. Video, correctly done, highly optimizes your pages for visibility.

Isn't Your goal to get those Eyeballs on Your Website, Google Places, Google + , and FaceBook to drive traffic to your business? Your Facebook Fan Page, now TimeLine, will act as a catalyst to acquire new customers. How would you like that? What do more customers mean? ... More Money!

Short Videos are the most engaging. 30 second to one minute Videos of yourself demonstrating or teaching something and then directing them to your website for your products or services is very effective. Or, you can direct them to your FaceBook TimeLine where you can capture their name and personal information. We market your business via video through many sources, - YouTube, AOL, Craigslist, FaceBook, etc.

Videos are fun. It takes only minutes to post it to YouTube. It is the optimization that is critical for your Video to go Viral. You can even post it with your smart phone in minutes. Posting it on YouTube, FaceBook, Twitter, etc. will have a Viral Effect. Now, how do you like that for inexpensive, Awesome Viral Marketing? When you post it on FaceBook, it goes from you to all your contacts, it travels to all of their contacts and so the dominos roll in your favor!

The **KEY** to keeping the person **engaged** is to keep your video short, interesting, informative and entertaining.

By leveraging these great resources you can use Your Website, Social Media, and Video to drive new business, create awareness, and become engaged with your target audience. You'll be able to take advantage and Create great Social Media friendly content to build the Know, Like and Trust Authority inexpensively.

Utilizing Video and using advanced optimization on the Videos, Website and Social Media platforms not only get the Eyeballs and traffic of the customer, but are sure to get Google's attention for ranking your site higher! We call it the **Next Gen YouTube Marketing.**

The smartest marketers in the world are crushing it with simple, inexpensive, easy to do video marketing as a part of their Blueprint Strategies.

Way 9

Step 6 of the 8 Step System

LinkedIn

LinkedIn is a business – related social networking site. It is primarily used for professional networking, focused on interactions and relationships of a business nature rather than personal, non-business engagement. As of January 2013, LinkedIn reported more than 200 million registered users in more than 200 countries and territories. Quantcast reports LinkedIn has 33.9 million monthly unique U.S. visitors and 47.6 million globally. In June 2011, LinkedIn had 33.9 million unique visitors, up 63 percent from a year earlier (2010) and surpassing MySpace according to Wikipedia. According to Mashable Business, Brian Hernandez, March 3, 2012, "LinkedIn sees 107 million unique monthly visitors"

LinkedIn, which might give off an air of humility and modesty, may fool you. However, it is obvious that as a social network for professionals, the people who use LinkedIn have an average income of $109,000 according to Mashable.

Of the 200 million active users, 2 new users every second, 77% of them are over 25. So, most of these individuals have gone to college and have secured a professional career.

Most people use LinkedIn to "get to someone" in order to make a sale, form a partnership, or get a job. It works well for this because it is an online network of more than 200 million experienced professionals from around the world representing 130 industries. However, it is a tool that is under-utilized, so I've compiled a top-ten list of ways to increase the value of LinkedIn.

Five Ways Guy Suggests to Use LinkedIn

Increase your visibility.

By adding connections, you increase the likelihood that people will see your profile first when they're searching for someone to hire or do business with. In addition to appearing at the top of search results (which is a **major plus** if you're one of the 52,000 product managers on LinkedIn), people would much rather work with people who their friends Know and Trust.

Improve your connect ability.

Most new users put only their current company in their profile. By doing so, they severely limit their ability to connect with people. You should fill out your profile like it's an executive bio, so include past companies, education, affiliations, and activities.

You can also include a link to your profile as part of an email signature. The added benefit is that the link enables people to see all your credentials, which would be awkward if not downright strange, as an attachment.

Improve your Google PageRank.

LinkedIn allows you to make your profile information available for search engines to index. Since LinkedIn profiles receive a fairly high PageRank in Google, this is a good way to influence what people see when they search for you.

To do this, create a public profile and select "Full View." Also, instead of using the default URL, customize your public profile's URL to be your actual name. To strengthen the visibility of this page in search engines, use this link in various places on the web. For example, when you comment in a blog, include a link to your profile in your signature.

Enhance your search engine results.

In addition to your name, you can also promote your blog or website to search engines like Google and Yahoo!

Your LinkedIn profile allows you to publicize websites. There are a few pre-selected categories like "My Website," "My Company," etc. If you select "Other" you can modify the name of the link. If you're linking to your personal blog, include your name or descriptive terms in the link, and voila! instant search-engine optimization for your site. *To make this work, be sure your public profile setting is set to "Full View."*

Ask for advice.

LinkedIn's newest product, LinkedIn Answers, aims to enable this online. The product allows you to broadcast your business-related questions to both your network and the greater LinkedIn network. The premise is that you will get more high-value responses from the people in your network than from open forums.

For example, here are some questions an entrepreneur might ask when the associates of a venture capital firm come up blank:

- Who's a good, fast, and cheap patent lawyer?
- What should we pay a VP of biz dev.?
- Is going to a Demo worth it?
- How much traffic does a TechCrunch plug generate?

Because of the high-income of the LinkedIn users, this is an ideal location for advertising for those businesses looking to profit from these kinds of cash-rich users. Yet, needless to say, even though LinkedIn's users are at the high end of the income bracket, it also caters to pretty much all income types.

According to Ryan Holmes CEO at HootSuite,

"Last year, Harvard Business Review surveyed 2,100 companies (*http://hbr.org/web/slideshows/social-media-what-most-companies-dont-know/2-slide*) and found that 79 percent use or plan to use social media. But a mere 12 percent of those firms felt they were using social media effectively. 2013 should see this frustrating gap between social media hype and reality begin to close as new social technologies take root. Companies institutionalize social practices and improved analytical tools show the real ROI on social investments."

The question is…**Are YOU On LinkedIn?** Not just haphazardly set up, but **Fully Optimized** to take advantage of the opportunities that may come forth from this network?

The **KEY** point to Remember is ... when playing on LinkedIn, you are playing on the professional platform.

Way 10

Step 7 of the 8 Step System

Mobile Enabled Website ...

Is Yours?

Your Mobile Opportunity

Bigger, Faster, Better than the Web

How many times have you wondered ... **"What did I ever do before the web?"** Soon we will be asking the same thing about our **Mobile Devices**.

The **Web Revolution** created the next generation of giants — companies like Google, Amazon, and eBay went from nothing to multi-billion dollar market caps in less than a decade. Today, **Mobile** is helping to fuel a new generation of giants — companies like Facebook, Groupon, and Zynga which have reached multi-billion dollar valuations in half the time of their predecessors ... and all without an IPO.

The **Mobile Revolution** will be like its web predecessor with two important exceptions:

- **M**obile will be more transformative than the web ... because your customers always have their **Mobile Devices** with them.
- **M**obile is going to evolve at a much faster pace ... because we've become proficient with our web experience. In fact, mobile shipments outpaced desktop/laptop shipments last year. **The race is on.**

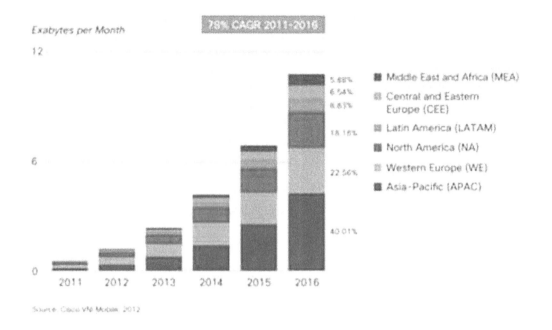

Exabytes per Month

78% CAGR 2011-2016

- Middle East and Africa (MEA)
- Central and Eastern Europe (CEE)
- Latin America (LATAM)
- North America (NA)
- Western Europe (WE)
- Asia-Pacific (APAC)

Source: Cisco VNI Mobile, 2012

With 69% of the searches done being from a Mobile device, are you losing that business because your site is not Mobile enabled? Does the potential customer become frustrated and move on to the next Google Place, now Google + recommendation on the list?

I hope not!

Advertising on Mobile - Recent Statistics

Mobile Local Advertising Dollars Projected To Surge Through 2017

Based on BIAKelsey's report, "**Mobile will be the fastest growing channel in the local advertising media market through 2017**". Their predicted share of local advertising earnings in 2017 is 7.1 %, an incredible boost from 1.7% this year. Location-targeted Mobile advertising spend is projected to surpass national ad dollars spent on mobile with this high-speed pace of growth.

With the Ad dollars being invested in mobile, due to the Mobile takeover, it is predicted to double this year to an estimated $2.9 billion, it is anticipated that Mobile Local Ad spend will flourish to approximately $10.1 billion by 2017.

Are you invested and infused in Mobile Marketing with your advertising? Or, will your company fall to the wayside?

PricewaterhouseCoopers estimated $3.4 billion would be spent on Mobile Geo location-targeted advertising in 2013, when in fact, the real number spent was $3.65 billion.

By 2017, researchers project that Geo Location-Targeted Mobile advertising spending will reach $9.1 billion, however, with the consistent growth it very well may exceed that expectancy.

Does your site look like this on Mobile   OR   LIKE THIS?

Courtesy of themedhb.com Courtesy of allrecipes.com

Do you realize that 40% of searches done are for restaurants? So, if you have a restaurant, it is almost mandatory that **You use a mobile site for Your restaurant**. Most customers are getting their information from the internet before they determine what they want to eat and where they choose to go. These customers are looking for menus, hours, directions, and phone numbers.

You can also utilize a **QR Code to link to your restaurant's splash page** showing the specific specials being offered with a coupon perhaps. The customer shows their phone to the server in order to redeem the coupon special (which may be a free signature appetizer with purchase of 2 entrees or whatever the restaurant chooses to offer).

Is your site Mobile Enabled?

We are experts at this creation. We can help you.

530-823-0888

Way 11

Step 8 of the 8 Step System

The Now Affordable Mobile App for Your Business is Within Reach!

Image Courtesy of Jeff Mills

- To Compete, YOU need an App!
- **5.2 B**illion **P**hones and **G**rowing
- **M**obile Apps 38 – 58 Billion by 2016 with 399% increase expected!
- **A**pple paid out over $2.5 Billion to App owners!
- **100** Billion **"PUSH"** Notifications sent

An Example of a "PUSH" Notification

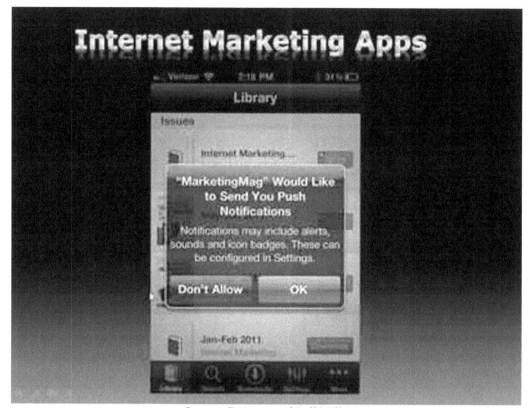

Image Courtesy of Jeff Mills

     Google acquired wireless phone maker Motorola Mobility for $12.5 billion, a Major deal to bolster adoption of Android to compete with Apple's IPhone.

Image Courtesy of Jeff Mills

BENEFITS TO LOCAL BUSINESSES

- **Engage Customers!**
- **GPS Directions and one Tap Calling**
- **"PUSH" Discount Offers and Coupons that pop up on their phone when sent (with your Mobile App your PUSH messages are free and unlimited…this can actually pay for the price of your Affordable MOBILE APP!)**
- **Menus, Reservations and Tip Calculator**
- **Viral Marketing – Built into the App – You Too Can Be On Itunes and the Android Market Place**
- **You are also "Front of Mind"/ Branding by your Icon Occupying Space on Their Phone**

Image Courtesy of Jeff Mills

- The Way people consume information is changing
- Mobile Devices and Tablets are taking over
- Companies are Transforming their Relationships with Customers
- Apps are replacing websites
- **Apps are Your Window of Opportunity to Revolutionize Your Business** as radically as the Web did
- We Now live in a Mobile World!
- It's Time … for **YOU** … to **Go Mobile!**

Mobile Apps are Affordable!

$495 for an Individual App

$1495 for a basic Business App

Plus a small monthly fee for licensing and maintenance.

Call 530-823-0888

Examples of the "App Look" on Your Phone

Always be in front of your Loyal Customer!

Image Courtesy of Jeff Mills

Image Courtesy of Jeff Mills

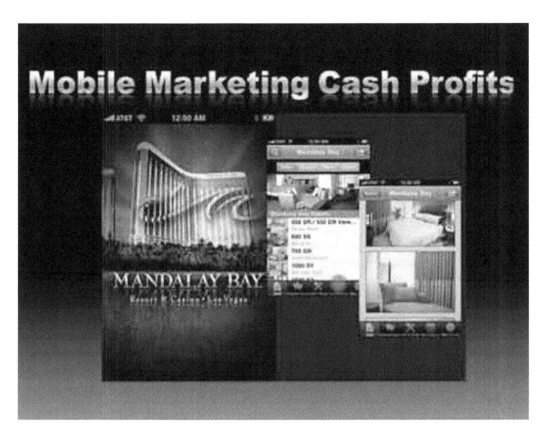

Image Courtesy of Jeff Mills

Image Courtesy of Jeff Mills

Even if You have an existing web presence, *You Won't want to miss this valuable information on how Your site can act as a Magnet for Search Engine Traffic and Drive Customers to You from their Mobile Devices.*

Get Access to More Details and Claim Your

Business Recognition!

Give us a call Today 530-823-0888 … to gain access

to more detailed information.

We'll also provide You information on how to take advantage of search marketing and social media to make your web presence viral in Today's Marketplace.

Way 12

A Strong, Engaging Call to Action is Imperative!

Ok, you have used some of these strategies and gotten them to your website.

Now, in order to entice them to Opt In, you must give them something of value for FREE. This Hook is known as your "Irresistible Offer".

You are simply making it irresistible for them. They really want your free video, report or whatever you are offering. So, they will happily complete the Opt In form providing you with their name and email address.

This is an integral part of your website, blog or Facebook fan page. You will now start building your list. It will mean the difference between getting one sale versus getting hundreds of sales through repeat business.

If you have not been successful at getting results with your ad copy, I suggest you hire an expert. You can also get great ideas by looking at popular magazines. Each headline of a magazine cover has excellent copywriting. It has a hook that makes people want to buy that magazine. You can use that for your own creative ideas!

Your take away to Remember here is …

"Call to Action" is Key!

Way 13

Get on Page 1 of Google Places Now Google +

Place Page Dominator.com will give You a Competitive Advantage!

What If I told you that You can be on the First Page of Google Places, now Google + whether You have a website or not? Yes, even if You have NO website!

The days of reaching Your potential customers with Yellow Pages, Print Media and other outdated methods are clearly numbered. *You need to be on the 1st Page of Google Places when someone is Searching to Buy Your Product or Service.*

Do You know **65%** of searches done are through **Smart Phones, IPhones, IPads** or other **Mobile Devices**? Being on the First Page of Google Places (Google +) in Your Market, **YOU** are out in **Front** of Your potential customers **24/7!**

1. To Rule Your Local Market Place, Place Page Dominator will Give You a Competitive Edge!

What if we get You on the Front Page of Google Places for Your Market Search?

- How would You like to Expand and Increase Your customer base?
- What if we Help You gain the advantage of reviews?
- Would You like to be found on **IPhones**, **Smart Phones**, **IPads**, and **GPS** devices?
- What if **You** can have the competitive edge on **Your** competition by being **one step ahead** of them?

Your **Google Places Business Listing** will contain vital information on Your business, such as hours of operation, coupons, special offers, contact information, and even interactive maps and driving directions.

If You already have a website, this too, is included. This **Magnetizes Search Engine Traffic** that funnels new customers to Your existing web presence.

Plus: When You purchase the **Place Page Dominator.com Package**, You'll…

2. Get First Page Google Ranking!

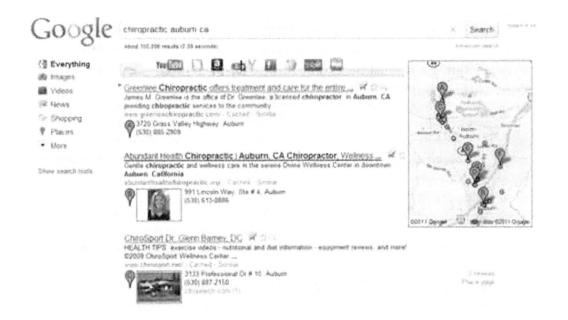

Business with 1st Page Rankings for their specific business type and location **Dominate the Search Engines.** *They are ultimately rewarded with new customers. (Remember implementing Video is a must!)*

It is our **Goal** to get You there! If You are already on **1st Page**, our **Goal** is to **Keep** You there.

With **65%** Searches being done with **Mobile Devices**, this is the <u>**Most Targeted Ever Advertising Your business can get**</u>. It reaches Your perfect customers at the **precise time** they are looking for information to purchase from Your type of business.

3. Leverage the Power of Being Recognized in Community Directories.

4. Automate Your Customer Testimonial.

We make it Easy by making available to You Social Igniter Cards if you don't have a Mobile App to encourage your customers to input a testimonial review on Google, Yelp, CitySearch, etc. **With Google's change in Algorithms, it is most necessary for the client to input a testimonial or review from the client's IP address, unique to them.** That can be their cell phone or home computer which is their personal address. Google frowns on all testimonials being done from 1 computer or IPad. Our goal is to systematically get you authentic, consistent positive reviews that do not appear as spam.

Don't Miss Out, Be The First In Your City!

FIND OUT more about PlacePageDominator.com Now!

- What if … we show You how Easy it is to get customer reviews?
- Ever wonder why You don't have more positive reviews? We can Help You with Reputation Repair.
- What if … I told You that we can get You on 1st Page of Google Places in Your Market, in Your City?
- Find out this vital information before Your competitors do.

Remember, the Key benefits to being on Page One of Google or other top search engines is that you get more traffic.

More Traffic = More Sales for Your Business

Get Access to More Details and Claim Your

Google Places, Google + Business Recognition!

Give us a Call and we'll give you a FREE analysis and we'll Personally Show You How!

CALL US Now!

916-900-2228

Way 14

Engage New Customers with Coupons & Savings

This is one of the most valuable ways to use Twitter, especially if you are a business owner or executive. For example, did you know that computer maker, Dell, by offering Twitter-only discounts, generated $3,000,000 in sales? That is right - $3,000,000 in sales in just one year alone!

It is very powerful to start using coupons and discounts for just your Twitter business community.

What you need to do in order to become successful is come up with special offers available only for your Twitter Followers.

Imagine the increase in sales you can have with just this alone! Think of the savings! Instead of printing coupons and spending Lots of money to send them in direct mailers to homes, imagine How much money you could Save with a 140-character line that is VIRTUAL and FREE!

- **Coupons:** According to CMS, a leading coupon processing agent, marketers issued 302 billion coupons in 2007, a 6% increase over the previous year. Over 76% of the population use coupons, according to the Promotion Marketing Association (PMA) Coupon Council. Coupons still work and provide an affordable marketing strategy for small business.

Attract Followers by Posting Free, Useful Information on Twitter

One of the very best approaches you can take to social media marketing is to disarm potential followers by providing something truly useful.

For instance, you could provide free information about something related to your niche, such as:

- Links to important news related to your niche, type of business
- Commentaries on important happenings within your niche, also
- Links to sales and coupons (even if they're not your own).

Once you use these strategies to build rapport with your visitors, you can then begin to reap the rewards by marketing various products to them.

Way 15

How Can You $ave 1000's in Advertising Dollars by Using a Special QR Code?

Turn Your Leads into Lifetime Customers

Know What a QR Code is? It's Like a Barcode on Steroids.

Know what it can do for You? Explode Your Offline Business!

Want Your Own QR Code?

Take ACTION NOW …

Give us a Call 916 – 900 - 2228

A QR Code (stands for "Quick Response") it is a mobile phone readable two-dimensional barcode that can be scanned by a smart phone's camera to transfer and store important information into your phone. This has been big in Japan forever, broke into Europe a while back, and is now gaining traction in the USA.

Check out both QR Codes

Scan them and see how QR Codes can work for Your Business!

Go Ahead. Check it out.

QR codes are similar to the barcodes you see in the supermarket and retail outlets. Barcodes track inventory and store price information. The key difference between the two is the amount of data they can hold or Bar share codes are linear one-dimensional codes and can only hold about 120 numerical digits, whereas QR codes are two-dimensional (2D) matrix barcodes that can hold thousands of alphanumeric characters of information. Their ability to hold more information and their ease of use makes them ideal for both small and large businesses.

In its simplest sense when someone scans or reads a QR code with an iPhone, Android or other camera-enabled Smartphone, by pointing their Smartphone at your QR Code it causes the phone to load data. If the device has had **QR Code decoding software** installed on it - **IPhone** *(https://itunes.apple.com/en/app/qr-code-reader-and-scanner/id388175979?mt=8)* or **Android** *(https://play.google.com/store/apps/details?id=la.droid.qr&hl=en)*, it will fire up its browser and go straight to that URL. When you scan you can do lots of things.

It is absolutely **A**MAZING! We can create **Y**our Custom **QR C**ode to do any of the following:

1. Browse to your Website – Using QRCodePowers.com's QR Code Service, people can scan your QR Code and automatically link to a webpage of your choice for more info about your product.

2. Link directly to a specific page of digital content on the web, such as your webpage, Squeeze Page or Facebook FanPage TimeLine, Google Places + page to lead them to give a review, etc.!

3. Bookmark a Website

4. Make a Phone Call for you with one touch dialing capability

5. Send a SMS Text Message

6. Send an Email

7. Create a VCard – Business Card with your contact information to the user to be stored instantly

8. Create an ECard

9. Create a Calendar Event

10. Google Map

11. Bing Map

12. Geographical Coordinates

13. YouTube URL for IOSs

14. Tweet on Twitter Free

15. Formatted Text Message — You can also setup a QR Code that when scanned automatically composes a text message with your keyword and short code so that all someone needs to do is press SEND to join your mobile list. An automated text message can be sent back to them with a special coupon or offer, and you automatically store their mobile numbers in your database with their instant authorization for you to text them later. Wow! Is that a Benefit you would like to add to your Marketing Strategy?

Any of these functions are easily achieved with Your QR Code.

FACTS

- **FACT**: 2010 saw a 1600% increase in number of QR Codes scanned. According to Daniel Mickens, QR Code Scans Skyrocketed in Q2 of 2012. "A recent mobile barcode trend report released by ScanLife showed huge growth in mobile barcode scanning. The trend report for Q2 of 2012 showed a record breaking number with 5.3 million scans In the month of June alone, the highest ever number of scans in a month."

- **FACT**: On average, a unique user scans 2-3 barcodes per month.

- **FACT**: 48 percent of mobile device owners surveyed made a purchase via their mobile phone.

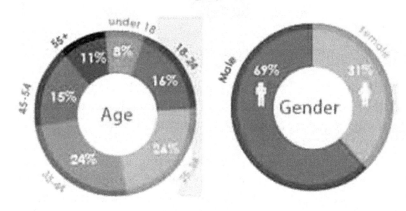

Source: http://www.clickz.com/clickz/news/2197586/qr-code-scans-skyrocket-in-q2-2012

It is key for marketers to focus on the demographics of QR Code users, especially with the increasing numbers. As you can see in the graph 69% of those who scan are men.

TOP QR CODE CAMPAIGNS'

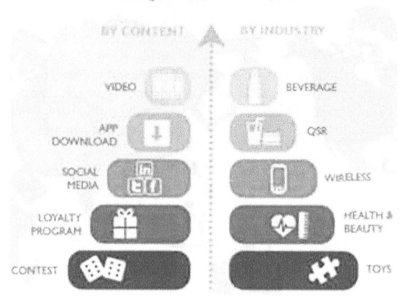

Source: http://www.clickz.com/clickz/news/2197586/qr-code-scans-skyrocket-in-q2-2012

The toy industry was the top industry followed by health and beauty. Wireless fell in at third and fast food restaurants followed. The beverage industry rounded out the top five industry campaigns.

The cool thing is ... Are you starting to see the power in this? **It's the business card of TODAY...but way better! No messing around writing down or typing your information into your phone, they just snap a picture of your QR Code with their phone and PRESTO! ... It's on their phone like magic!** Pretty awesome ... Great for Marketing to expose your business!!!

The future of targeted Marketing rests in the palm of your hand. QR Codes & Mobile Marketing ... Visit these sites:

http://www.PlacePageDominator.com or http://www.QRCodePowers.com unite your products with customers via their iPhone, android phone, Blackberry, Windows Mobile, and hundreds of other mobile phones in use today.

YOU can Track your marketing dollars and sales with the http://www.PlacePageDominator.com campaign management system.

We can quickly put QR Codes to work for you. As a business, your bottom line is, well, your bottom line! **Increase exposure, Increase sales, Increase revenue.**

No other medium can match the power and potential that smartphones represent in today's economy. Television, radio, and print marketing all hold fast and true to the "call to action" methodology for driving sales. The difference with QR Barcode marketing lies in the ability for the consumer to **TAKE ACTION at the point of contact!**

So, what lies ahead? That is the million dollar question and the one that businesses, large and small are scrambling to answer. Those who think out of the box and use these technologies in new and creative ways to engage customers are the ones that will reap huge rewards. **Those who "Wait and See" will be playing catch up.**

Mobile Marketing is here now and the use of QR Codes will be the force that drives it!

At this point I'm guessing you see the **Power** in this.

Want Your Own QR Code?

http://www.QRCodePowers.com

Take ACTION NOW!

Give us a Call 916 - 900 – 2228

This could be *Your QR Co*de on

Your customer's phone

Get with the 21st Century! Be on the Cutting Edge.

ASK us about our most effective QR Code TRACKING System. You'll love it!

Beat your competition.

Way 16

Turn Those Browsers into Buyers

You are in business, right? Are you an Attorney, Dentist, Chiropractor, Furniture Store, Restaurant, Plastic Surgeon, Weight Loss Coach, Liposuction Plastic Surgeon, Plumber, Heating and Air Conditioning Service, Jeweler, Veterinary, Horse Trainer, or Car Dealership? All businesses need to step up and realize that Advertising has been revolutionized!

Do you need to Take Action and Step Into the 21st Century of Marketing to be on the cutting edge? What do you think will happen to your business if you keep using the same old methods of advertising from the past and Your Competition steps up far before you do?

Who will be the most seasoned and strongest on Google and who will need to play catch up? Time will work against you. Seasoning is Power.

That's why you want to use Social Media for your business and for yourself. Not only do you want to Brand Yourself, but you want to get all the individuals who are interested in what you have to say, into your sales funnel.

That way you can **turn** Browsers into Buyers and market to them times over and over again.

So how do you turn Browsers into Buyers?

HERE'S HOW!

You should use an automated lead capture system. Wouldn't you want a 24-7 virtual employee working for your business? You can do that by using such marketing systems as Get Response, Aweber, or Constant Contact.

This helps you stay connected with your prospects and customers.

You can do this yourself, or have a marketing company, as MarkeingMobileUSA.com *(http://www.marketingmobileusa.com/)* is, help you implement this. You can have a Strategic BluePrint created for your specific goals.

Feel free to contact Marketing Mobile USA.com

at (530) 823 – 0888 to help you Brand your company and products.

Way 17

Explosive Viral Loop 24/7 Marketing System

Do you realize Your

Social Media Assets Are of

Monetary Value to your business?

When you start creating social media sites for yourself or your company, you are creating assets that you can sell in the future! Yes, these are Salable ASSETS.

Let's look at the blogging explosion we've seen over the last few years. The movie "Julie and Julia" opened the world's eyes about the power of blogging. It took blogging mainstream for many who had no idea that an average person could get attention, socialize with the world and pursue their passion using a simple blogging platform available to the masses for free!

Let's take a look at just some successful 'Blog It and Sell It" stories: "The Bankaholic blog was sold for $15 million. ArsTechnica sold for $25 million. PaidContent sold for $30 Million" per Maria Gudelis.

Way 18

Is It Necessary to Respond to Bad Reviews?

Reputation Management

YES, Respond to Bad Reviews.

Using the Twitter Search Engine, try to find all instances where your products and services have been mentioned. In particular, look for bad reviews of your products, complaints about customer service, and generally anything else that is negative.

Once you locate these negative comments, make it a priority to respond to each of them individually. Engaging in the conversation is your way of being able to hopefully resolve the issue before it escalates. You can also do this by providing free products to those with complaints, or by offering to redress the problems they have (if this is possible).

If you find that people are complaining about a certain feature of your product, then you may want to consider fixing it (if it is sufficiently inexpensive)—you may want to then re-release it for free to those who have already purchased.

Using the recommended strategies above, you should be able to turn any negative press you find into positive press. People are likely to say good things about you and your company after you redress the problems or offer compensation.

Balance Your Customers & Your Time

As a business owner, you value your time greatly. You know that every move you make impacts the productivity of the entire business—not just your own. This is why it is so important for you to cautiously make time-allocation decisions.

When it comes to social media marketing, most would argue that you should err on the side of over-engagement, rather than under-engagement. I agree with this; however, I would suggest that you take steps to automate procedures and to engage customers efficiently through this process.

You should treat your Social Media Marketing efforts like a true Marketing Campaign. If you were wasting an inordinate amount of time across any other dimension with your business (and weren't getting any return from it), you'd either change your approach or find more ways to be efficient with your current approach...**And** that is exactly what you should do here, too.

We are Experts at Reputation Management. However, it is a challenging marketing task, which the Key is to catch it early and resolve the problems. Or, **in some cases**, it has been our experience that it is necessary ***to improve the attitude or work ethics of your staff,*** such as answering the phone on 2 or 3 rings with a happy attitude. We do not want to fix the pot holes only for more to quickly appear.

Way 19

Integrate Your Social Media Marketing With Everything Else

Rather than using your Twitter and Facebook accounts in total isolation from the rest of your business, think about using them in a way that complements your current business model. Create a Facebook Business Page *(It cannot be your Personal Page).* With our specific Facebook template, there are ways of using it as a Traffic Magnet to draw new customers and clients.

Image Source: boringem.org, nadinemuller.org.uk

For instance, if you use print advertising, you might consider using it to channel traffic to your social networking site profiles where, with Facebook's new timeline, you can display your particular product or service in the image icons.

Or consider this example: It has become common practice for television news programs to refer watchers to company-specific (and reporter) Facebook profiles and Twitter profiles. The reason for this is simple. By getting people to follow them through social networking sites, those news stations gain yet another point through which they can advertise and engage watchers. You … can do the same!

If you use this strategy correctly, you could significantly boost the results from your other marketing campaigns by filtering visitors through your network.

This will allow you to capture visitors by getting them to join your network, so that you can repeatedly pitch to them often (rather than only once) in a low-pressure atmosphere.

Way 20

Remember that Social Media Marketing is Still Marketing!

At the end of the day, your goal for all Social Media projects should be to earn a favorable return. Now, this return might not be immediate and it may take months or even a year to realize even combining various methodologies. But, with that said, your goal should still be a return.

It is best for you to start now rather than allowing your competition to be on the cutting edge and leaving you in the dust struggling to catch up. YOU want to be the one on the cutting edge and ahead of your competitors. **Don't let the competition take your business because the customer searched their needs on their phone and You don't appear!**

With that in mind, think about how you can make your Social Media Marketing ventures more profitable. One way you can do this is to cut down on the amount of time you spend doing things that aren't profitable.

For instance, on a daily basis, you might receive Facebook friend requests, Twitter follower requests, and other requests; however, rather than processing each one as it becomes available; you should think about doing it on a weekly (or at most a daily basis). Allot 15 to 30 minutes a day to interact with your Facebook Fan Page. With some of our "Push Button" features, this is possible.

Alternatively, you might consider using social networking sites with your mobile phone while waiting in an office for an appointment, thus saving you time.

This will allow you to make requests, accept requests, and perform updates when you have free time, but are not near a computer.

Let me Help You create and manage your video blog, all with push-button simplicity so you can leverage this influence-engine giant for your benefit…And increase your bottom line year after year.

Way 21

Pinterest

The Latest & Greatest Viral

24/7 Social Media!

Simply stated, Pinterest is a content sharing service that allows members to "pin" images, videos and other objects to their pinboard. It also includes standard social networking features.

The beauty of Pinterest lies in its simplicity. The site harnesses the power of the personal referral. By creating topic-specific pinboards, you can organize and share the things you love with others, in a visually pleasing way. You also can browse pinboards created by other people to discover new foods, products, adventures and opportunities, to be inspired by those who share your interests.

Pinterest has opened an entirely new door for businesses to use the internet inside the traffic funnels and referral based strategies.

According to James Lawrence, "Pinterest is the fastest growing site in history to break 10 million unique visits in one week. In December of last year it entered the top 10 social networks ranked by visits, and in January this year it drove more traffic to online retailers than LinkedIn, YouTube and Google+ combined. Few social media properties have enjoyed such explosive growth and general buzz."

So, what Is Pinterest according to James?

Pinterest describes itself as a "Virtual pinboard to organize and share the things you love". In simple terms you create an account and can 'pin' media that you find around the net to a series of image boards. In essence image boards are categories of images. As an account owner you can maintain a range of boards on any topic of interest. You can pin images to a particular board either by uploading content from your computer, or using a Pinterest plug-in on your browser to pin content from any website you visit back to your board (provided you comply with

Pinterest's terms & conditions). These boards can be viewed by friends, and other users, who can then re-pin media appearing on your board to their own.

Does It Matter For Businesses?

Pinterest is receiving a significant amount of commercial hype due to the way it engages users.

As of January 2012, "ComScore.com found that Facebook is the time-sucking champion, averaging 405 minutes per visitor in the month of January, but **Tumblr** and **Pinterest** managed to capture a significant 89 minutes of our time.

Twitter came in fourth place with 21 average minutes, but that number has less to do with attraction to the service and more to do with the fact that ComScore.com did not include mobile usage in any of its data and looked solely at Twitter.com"

http://www.businessreviewusa.com/marketing/social-media/how-much-time-do-we-spend-on-social-media-sites

The Diagram to the right or below, published by the Wall Street Journal

Notes: World-Wide data Does Not Include Mobile Usage. Twitter.com data only. Source: ComScore.com.

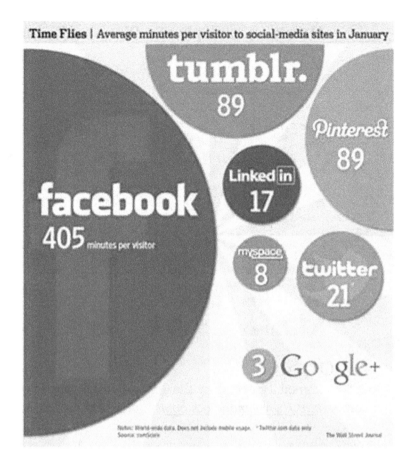

Time Flies | Average minutes per visitor to social-media sites in January

tumblr. 89

Pinterest 89

facebook 405 minutes per visitor

Linked in 17

myspace 8

twitter 21

3 Go gle+

But, like most new Social Media phenomenon the jury is still out as to what kind of real impact Pinterest can have to the bottom line of most businesses.

The visual nature of the network means that product companies, especially in creative spaces, should be able to leverage the network to have their content shared.

In the USA, companies like Kate Spade *(http://pinterest.com/source/katespade.com/)*, Whole Foods *(http://pinterest.com/wholefoods/)* and Gap *(http://pinterest.com/source/gap.com/)* have quickly taken to the network and have seen large numbers of users follow their boards.

We would advise business owners with great visual content to start engaging with the Pinterest network.

If you do engage, with all social media properties, be careful to balance self-promotion with providing users with interesting and engaging content.

Remember, it is all about the USER and you will also gain the benefit.

Here's an example of a Pinterest Pinboard.

ModCloth joined Pinterest in the Fall of 2011, but it's already one of ModCloth.com's *(http://www.modcloth.com/)* top unpaid referral sites in terms of traffic and revenue. Why? According to Barnes, it's thanks to "product photography and blog content that resonates with their audience." ModCloth has approximately 7,000 pins tagged on Pinterest, and 99% of them are from advocates of the ModCloth brand and products, she adds.

Ideas For Luring Massive Followers

To gain massive followers, it is necessary to intertwine with other feeds to borrow from the viral juices of the various other Social Medias. Try applying these ideas to your own Pinterest profile and watch your number of followers soar! What surge of followers do you think you'll get if you try these suggestions?

Tip #1 – Tie Fans into a Contest as in this ModCloth Example On Facebook

"Whether you seek outfit advice or tips on what's in-trend, the ModStylists *(http://www.modcloth.com/modstylists)* are your go-to gals. But, they wanted you to show off what excellent ensembles you could come up with for their Fall Fashions, "Styled by You Contest".

Between 9 a.m. PT on 7/30 and 3 p.m. PT on 8/3, go to the **ModStylist Facebook Fan Page** *(http://www.facebook.com/modstylists),* this was where you could put together your fave fall-fabulous look using a Polyvore Mini Editor app loaded with autumn-appropriate ModCloth items.

Once the contest ended, the ModStylists chose five winners to receive a **$100 gift certificate.** Not only that, but the selected lucky ModFans worked with the ModStylists to **create two outfits each for a "Shop Our Outfits"** feature on ModCloth!" per ModCloth online contest.

Now that sounds like Fun! And, the creator of the outfit gets recognition. Who knows, like the Apprentice Show, this may land someone a new career."

Now was that an ingenious idea? What better way to engage your present followers and gain new followers by their viral excitement and getting their friends to also join the contest.

Tip #2 – Tie Into Your Existing Social Networks

Try tying in your existing Facebook and Twitter profiles to get Pinterest followers. This has proven to be the fastest way. By doing this, every new item you pin will also be displayed to your followers on those networks. Since you have already established relationships with subscribers on Facebook and Twitter, you'll find that many of them will elect to follow your Pinterest profile naturally. Not only that, but, when your friends join, Pinterest will make them Auto-Follow you. Hmmmmmmmm… Isn't that Sweet?

Tip #3 – Make it Easy to Pin Your Content

Do you want new followers for your profile? Integrating **Pinterest buttons** into your blog posts, product pages and other areas of your site can help boost the number of times your content is pinned. This leads to new followers for your profile. Since Pinterest is still relatively new, by having Pinterest buttons in place provides a visual reminder for people to subscribe to your profile and engage with your Pinterest content.

Tip #4 – Create Boards to Supplement Your Posts

Alternatively, why not create a Pinterest board that's built around one of your blog posts? For example, if you are a **Veterinary**, you can recommend several different products or preventive maintenance treatments for their pets in a new blog post. Create a Pinterest board tied to this post that shares these recommendations in a visual way. Some people comprehend in a visual manner.

If you are a **Restaurant**, share enticing pictures of the prepared selections on your Menu.

If you are a **Realtor**, share your listings and post the price tag banner on each Listing. Offer maintenance tips in a video. Doing these things make your content more valuable and engaging, giving readers a reason to follow your profile.

If a **Car Dealership**, share your available cars and post the price tag banner on each Listed. Offer tips in a video of various car maintenance to attract them.

If a **Weight Loss Consultant** or a **Plastic Surgeon** entice your clients to share the Before and After photos by Offering them a Contest for doing so.

Tip #5 – Pin Regularly –Consistency is Key

As with any Social Media site, determining how often to pin new content involves finding the ideal threshold between posting so little that there's no value in following your profile and posting so often that people get annoyed with your constant updates.

Strategized properly, Campaigns should Average 10 – 23 Pins per day with an Average of 15 – 32 unique followers and relevant traffic to your blog.

Pinterest – Happy Pinning

For Ultimate Prosperity.

Conclusion

Top 5 Ways <u>You</u> Should Be Promoting Your Business Online

I hope I have given you some fresh ideas about how you can leverage the power of many different social media platforms to attract new customers and drive sales to your current business to increase profits in this economy.

With our expertise at MarketingMobileUSA.com *(http://MarketingMobileUSA.com)*, we create a Strategic BluePrint implementing many different ways for You to use the internet to your advantage to increase profits, promote and brand yourself and your services online…Here are my all-time favorites:

#1 SOCIAL MEDIA MARKETING

As we have touched on in this book, because of social networks people have changed the way they research and make buying decisions.

As of the last quarter of 2012, "Facebook now has more than 1 billion people using the service in a given month, 29 percent more than a year ago. Yes, 1,000,000,000!'

The company said **543 million** of them accessed the service through a **mobile device,** a 67 percent increase."

Facebook is a giant of 1,000,000,000 (1 billion) users that cannot be ignored!

FaceBook Revealed on January 29, 2014 the following:

- 1.23 Billion Monthly Active Users (16% Increase)
- 945 Million Active Mobile Monthly Users (+39%)
- 296 Million Mobile-Only Active Users (+Doubled in last year)
- Mobile Ad Revenue Now at 1.25 Billion
- Total Ad Revenue Now at 2.34 Billion

When leveraged in your favor you'll have the opportunity to build more trust, respect, and credibility than ever before.

Imagine being able to have feedback on how to improve your business and sell more on a daily basis. Or through a Contest finding out just what people would like to see and buy, which having this knowledge leads you to PROFITS.

And just imagine being able to turn every customer into your potential raving fan who will advertise for you. I can make that happen for your business, and you can secure my services exclusively in your local market.

According to SocialBakers.com

"The Socialbakers team was excited to hear Facebook's results from it's Q2 earnings call last night. Facebook is performing exceptionally well, and we've summarised some of the key points so that you can see what's interesting from an advertising and user perspective.

- Facebook has 1.155 billion users – an increase of 45 million users
- Mobile monthly active users has grown by 51% last year to 819 million – 219 million are mobile only!
- Mobile daily active users are at 469 million users
- Revenue in Q2 2013 was $1.81 billion, of which $1.59 billion was from advertising
- 41% of all advertising revenue came from mobile advertising – this is a huge jump compared to last quarter's 30% figure

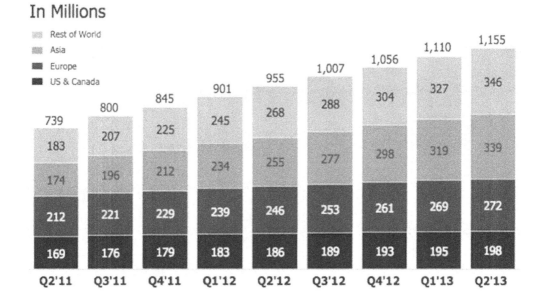

Source: Socialbakers.com

Other Interesting Facts:

- 5 million videos were uploaded on Instagram in just the first day alone
- Facebook has 1 million active advertisers (getting the Average budget per advertiser to $1590 per quarter) – interesting stats if you apply the 80:20 rule

- 100 million monthly active users use the app, "Facebook for Every Phone" for native phones (intended to reach audiences where smartphones are not yet generally affordable)

Regional Facebook Monthly Active Users Split is:

Rest of World (Africa, LATAM) – 346 million users

Asia – 339 million users

Europe – 272 million users

US & Canada – 198 million users

Mobile is skyrocketing and these Facebook stats prove it. In fact, 41% of Facebook revenue comes from mobile! This is truly amazing!"

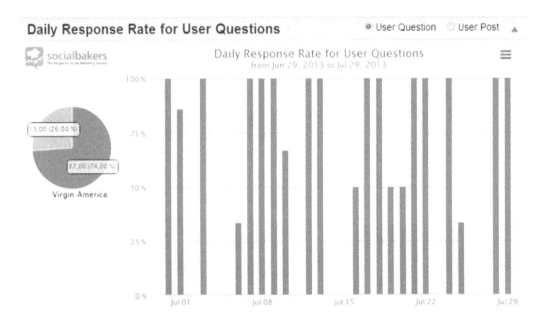

Source: Socialbakers.com

#2 VIDEO MARKETING

Would you believe that, according to Mashable.com in January 2012, YouTube serves up 5 BILLION videos to viewers per month in the United States alone? While in May, YouTube reached an all-time high of 14.6 Billion videos viewed! What's more, YouTube is the #4 search engine on the internet, which means that <u>right now</u> somebody is likely searching for your services online in the form of a video.

As of January 2013, according to the article done by Kostas Kostalampros in the Search Engine Journal, YouTube is NOW the 2nd largest search engine after Google. It has over four billion hours of video watched each month. What a difference a year has made!

Imagine if you had the budget to run infomercials 24 hours a day, 7 days a week…you'd dominate your market. That's the power of video marketing.

Let me show you how this is possible on a low budget (even in a terrible economy!), and how to engender more trust and respect with your customers than ever before.

Here are some statistics of how YouTube is a powerful growing source for you to be seen and branded.

Google Sites are driven primarily by video viewing at YouTube.com, ranked as the top online video content property in March posting the highest average engagement among the top ten video properties.

Now, only **2** months later… (back to the statistics of 2012) May 2012

According to ComScore article, as of June 24, 2012, "183 million U.S. Internet users watched online video during the month of May compared to 178 million in April. ComScore reports that YouTube saw record viewership in May with an all-time high of 14.6 Billion videos viewed and surpassing the threshold of 100 videos **per viewer** for the first time. The report also showed that 144.1 million viewers watched 14.6 billion videos on YouTube.com (which works out to 101.2 videos per viewer).

In May, U.S. Internet users watched nearly 34 billion videos, with Google Sites taking the top spot with 14.6 billion videos, representing 43.1 percent of all videos viewed online. ComScore says that YouTube accounted for the vast majority of videos viewed at the property. Hulu came in second with 1.2 billion videos, or 3.5 percent of all online videos viewed, a slight increase from April.

Microsoft Sites ranked third with 642 million (1.9 percent), followed by Vevo with 430 million (1.3 percent) and Viacom Digital with 347 million (1.0 percent).

According to the release, 84.8 percent of the total U.S. Internet audience viewed online video. The average Hulu viewer watched 27.0 videos, totaling 2.7 hours of video per viewer. The duration of the average online video was 4.3 minutes.

In terms of number of viewers, nearly 183 million viewers watched an average of 186 videos per viewer in May. Google Sites attracted 144.6 million unique viewers during the month (101.2 videos per viewer), followed by Yahoo Sites with 46.0 million viewers (7.3 videos per viewer), and Vevo with 45.6 million viewers (9.4 videos per viewer).

What is your opinion? Is creating your own VIDEO Channel important to Brand and Expose your business, services and products? Do you think You Can Profit by being seen 24 hours a day on YouTube leading the viewer from Your YouTube Channel to Your Website?

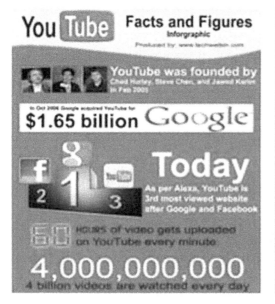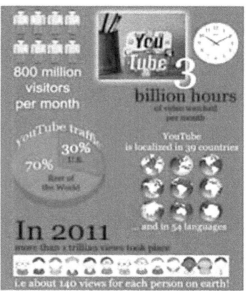

http://www.jeffbullas.com/2012/05/23/35-mind-numbing-youtube-facts-figures-and-statistics-infographic/

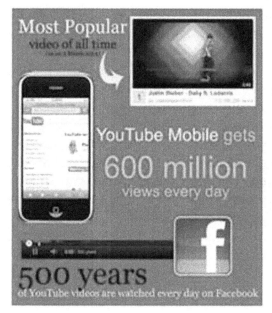

http://www.jeffbullas.com/2012/05/23/35-mind-numbing-youtube-facts-figures-and-statistics-infographic/

#3 LEAD-CAPTURE & FOLLOW-UP CAMPAIGNS

Did you know that even a GREAT webpage will only convert 5% of its visitors to a purchase?

It's absolutely true, and this means that 19 out of 20 visitors to your website are destined to surf away into the ether…and very likely find your competitor's website instead.

But consider this: the AVERAGE page that offers consumers' free information in exchange for their contact info gets 35-40% conversion.

Imagine being able to instantly increase your return on leads 7-FOLD, and do it with push- button automation just with the right positioning and Call to Action.

This is all very possible, and I can show you.

#4 LOCAL SEARCH VISIBILITY ON BOTH PCS AND MOBILE

Did you know that 30% of all searches online include a city or local term (like "Sacramento Plumbing Contractors")? And remember that 65% of the searches are done from a Mobile Device.

This means that every online search for goods and services will feature the local companies that have figured out how to get listed at the top of Google's page 1.

Of course, it goes without saying that your customers can't hire you if they **can't find you online**. Having a website is like driving on the freeway at 5 o'clock traffic you're in the gridlock with thousands of others. If you aren't exposed (and accelerating in the carpool lane) you won't ever be found, you'll be left sitting there chugging along. I can make sure that your local business is **found** on Google and other resources...for all of the keywords that you need to rank for so that your neighbors can find you online. Contact me at www.MarketingMobileUSA.com for your free Consultation.

#5 PINTEREST MARKETING INTERTWINED WITH THE OTHER SOCIAL MEDIAS

Did you know that 77% of all internet users follow one or more Social Media blogs such as, FaceBook, Twitter, Pinerest, etc.? If you're not capitalizing on this growing community, you're missing out on a huge amount of business.

Pinners on Pinterest appear to be passionate about sharing, and if you have them as clients and can turn them into raving fans, they can propel your business to new heights.

Let me help you create and manage your Pinterest picture and video virtual Pinboards, all with push-button simplicity so you can leverage this influence-engine giant for your benefit...And increase your bottom line year after year.

Pinterest Usage Statistics Infographic Highlights:

1. Pinterest users spend an average of almost 16 minutes on the site per visit (12.1 for Facebook).
2. 50% of Pinterest users have children.
3. Almost 70% of Pinterest users are female.
4. 97% of Pinterest's Facebook fans are women.
5. As of January 2012, Pinterest had received just under 12 million unique visits. As seen in Forbes Magazine, May 8, 2013, "Representatives from comScore say that Pinterest hosted 53.3 million unique visitors in March, roughly doubled its traffic from a year earlier. But just as important as growth, says Levine, is those users' engagement with the site. "People spend enormous amounts of time using it,"

6. Pinterest receives almost 1.5 million visitors each day.

Pinterest provides more referral traffic to other sites than Google+, YouTube and LinkedIn combined.

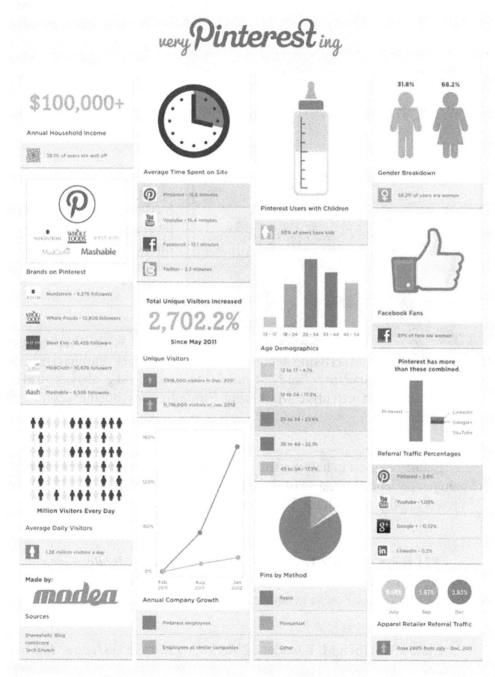

Source: Arson Alex

Having lived in Silicon Valley, Elaine has loved and been involved in the internet for over 2 decades. She is a Teacher, Lecturer and Advisor both domestically and internationally for more than 45 years.

Elaine Albright helps businesses, small and large to leverage and implement the marketing technology and methodology of the 21st Century.

With her expertise, utilizing the latest advertising techniques of the Internet, emphasizing Social Media, Video Marketing, and Mobile Marketing, she drives traffic by exploiting the most effective Marketing Strategies for businesses to achieve more Profits.

Elaine believes in helping solve these economic marketing challenges that are being experienced because of the lack of newspaper readers and the ability of TV viewers to flip through the TV commercials unwatched.

"21 Ways to Boost Your Business Profits Using Mobile, Video Marketing & Social Media Tools" teaches you to Embrace it, Be Engaged, which ultimately Empowers You to generate more income!

Elaine V. Albright, Founder of Marketing Mobile USA.com has been recognized for her Social Media, Mobile and Video Marketing expertise both in the United States and Internationally.

http://www.BoostYourBusinessProfitsUsingMobileVideoMarketingSocialMedia.com

http://www.MarketingMobileUSA.com,

MarketingMobileUSA@Gmail.com

or by leaving a voicemail on her dedicated

Client Hotline # 530-823-0888

(or you may even catch her if she is not on another line!). See if a partnership would be a good fit for your business.

Check out this QR Code

Women Entrepreneurs: Stop Struggling! Connect with Me. Uncover Easy Client Attraction Formulas & Entrepreneurs – explode your business = app development & Social Media.

For special discount information on bulk purchases, please contact

Marketing Mobile USA at 1-530 – 823 - 0888 or

MarketingMobileUSA@Gmail.com

Now What?

You deserve to be able to consume this content anywhere possible, on any device possible, and you have that opportunity when purchasing … *"21 Ways to Boost Your Business Profits Using Mobile, Video Marketing & Social Media Tools"*.

As I mentioned in the beginning of this book, we want to keep you posted on the Latest Marketing Trends to keep you in the loop. When you send your receipt to:

Bonuses@BoostYourBusinessProfitsUsingMobileVideoMarketingSocial Media.com

We will immediately send you your bonus, but you will also get a few other things that we will periodically email your way that will help you tremendously. You'll love them. How does that sound?

Please Email us your receipt now so we can help you on your Marketing journey that by simply implementing will increase Your Business Profits.

You'll love it.

Look forward to seeing your Marketing and Advertising … Stepping Into the 21st Century.

Cheers,

Elaine

www.ingramcontent.com/pod-product-compliance
Lightning Source LLC
Chambersburg PA
CBHW082110070326
40689CB00052B/4490